On Long Loan

Vanessa Lampert

First Published in 2020
By Live Canon Poetry Ltd
www.livecanon.co.uk

978-1-909703-45-2

A CIP catalogue record for this book is available from the British Library.

On Long Loan

Vanessa Lampert

Vanessa Lampert has an MA in Writing Poetry from Newcastle University and Poetry School London, graduating in 2019. In 2020 she won the Café Writers Prize and the Ver Prize and came second in the Fish Prize. She has been published in a number of magazines including *Magma*, *The Moth* and *The Interpreter's House*. She co-edits *The Alchemy Spoon*.

Vanessa lives in Oxfordshire where she works as an acupuncturist. This is her first pamphlet.

Acknowledgments

'Canada' was awarded first prize in the Café Writers Prize 2019
'Woodland' was awarded first prize in the Ver Prize 2020
'Margate in September' and 'What the horses told us' were shortlisted in the Bridport Prize 2020
'Shed' first appeared in *The Interpreter's House*
'Pneumonia' was highly commended in the Segora Prize 2020
'Curations' was highly commended in the Bridport Prize 2018
'The Song of it' appeared with the title 'Love' in *Bluehouse Journal*
An earlier version of 'Rain' first appeared in the Live Canon Anthology 2020

Contents

for Adam and Sophie

Not like this park

My park will be a bowl to hold sunlight,
the sky dropped on long loan. Shade
no one would need to call *the shadows*.
No crouching spikes of glass in grass by rusty swings,
no busted drinking fountain left for years,
no *Fuck off* gouged on a bench by an angry hand, no harm,
no drinking, no bargaining, or pleading with God for out.
My park will be the out, with a café painted yellow,
where we'll watch a woman in an apron
fill a cake with raspberries and whipped cream.
No dogs bred for menace, routinely whipped,
their owners beaten or broken. No men staring at Betfair on iPhones,
no polystyrene takeaway trays, no greasy paper
blowing over the grass like fallen cloud.
No bags of shit dangling from branches like baubles,
no man hanging, no police car, no yellow plastic tape pulled taut.
No note in a freezer bag tied to a tree, saying *babe oh why, the boys?*
No flowers left there cheap and dying, and drying
or already dead. My park will have great beds of roses, white roses,
their stems unbroken and no one to break them,
no one in my park but us. The warm
weight of your hand in my hand. High up there,
fistfuls of stars, all hidden, and us
not needing to wait until dark to know
they'll keep coming back.

Oh Jossers We

Josser: circus word for an outsider

Here come the circus folk, self-assured, lithe,
justifying summer with their thighs.
They're lighting up the village green like blossom.
Retro-chic and velvety, juggling old cutlery,
qualmless and oblivious to cold. See them
expertly erecting their marquees, pirouetting,
irresistible to doves. I almost ran away
to join them way back when. I had core strength
and was not shunned by ponies. Oh jossers we,
who have not clung to the trapeze, nor held aloft
a woman on one hand. We who failed
to sail through air while smiling wildly, now
must witness all this fearless allure.
See them safe inside their neon painted spandex,
shiny as a shoal of jubilant fish. If this be a dream
then hide the truth from me. There are so many
lovely things we can never hold or keep. I won't
be a girl again nor ever you a boy. Still they come
to mingle amongst us, jeopardy and tumbling,
hula-hooping, reaping what they sow. Oh come again,
restore us. Hang by your teeth and spin for us,
for we have loved you longer than our lives.

Wasps

Harmonious scheme of the good year
for apples and wasps. Fruit piled high
in roadside boxes, furious hover.

I'm learning to read, doing it aloud.
Oh gorgeous sound of the love I have
for me. 'COX'S. PLEASE HELP YOURSELF'.

Behind closed doors, matters ripen and rot.
My father packs the car. Backs it out fast,
I wave, can't know if he sees me or not.

Unscheduled rain digs its heels in hard.
Boxes swell to breaking point. Apples roll,
crushed under wheels that turn for somewhere,

warm smell of cider rising from the road.
My mother is stung and hollowed-out, I wait
out the back, watching wasps. Innocent crawl

and hum on windfalls, pitted with decay.
I watch their habits of enter and gorge,
how they rise to leave armed and I wait.

Dangle

Those times we caught the Oxford train,
I wished for a compartment to ourselves,
would slide open the heavy door hopeful
we might slip inside, so I could clamber
to dangle upside down from the luggage rack,
its cold chrome bar across the backs of my knees,
shouting *look at me Mum*, her laughing
while I swung, sandaled toes tucked for leverage
under the slats, my red ribboned plaits
reaching for the dusty seat, hem of my skirt
touching my chin, knickers on display,
caring nothing for the rules of good, polite,
of *kindly keep your feet off the seats,*
just swinging to and fro on a hurtling train,
heedless of the threat to *get down and stoppit,*
though we never once had a compartment
to ourselves, instead shared with men in suits,
the occasional obedient dog, old couples
wearing clothes too warm for the season,
and once a man in a blue rubber swimming hat,
tight with drink and eating a choc-ice that ran
and dripped its sticky cream onto his cuffs,
his chinos, but mostly women with children
like me, our hair clean and soft, sitting quietly,
eyeing each other, perhaps waiting, perhaps
longing for someone to break free, or only
savouring the journey, seeing Oxfordshire
slide by sideways, to arrive, brakes shrieking
over their shiny rails, and me, a woman
in her fifties standing to button her coat,
reaching to take down her bag from the rack,
its crossways slats robust, still possible.

Toads

I liked it when the road outside our old house was dotted
with toads, their eyes more golden than you'd think,
their bodies dry and low, all the colours of old leaves.
I asked a woman wearing serious shoes *what's happening?*
She said the toads were walking home to spawn,
that they did it every spring, brought the street to life,
toads all roaring the same *love me love me fuck me* call
that sounded like a marble rolling over hard ridged plastic.
I liked that the street was full of people in green tabards
marked TOAD PATROL, saving the toads
from cars, bending and lifting every living toad
singing as they ferried toads from danger,
casually dismantling peril in matching clothes.
They were my favourites, the ones that sang
You're gonna be alright. I liked that I had a woman
to ask questions of because I had so many. I was a girl
out on the street with my baby in a purple sling, crying.
I was just trying to soothe him with all I had
which, after milk, after clean and dry was to sing.
I sang *Toady toady too rye ay.* Did he cry less beneath the sky?
Maybe I imagined it because I wasn't alone out there,
toads and kindness and the weather finally turning warm.
I liked how people stopped traffic by raising an arm
looking certain, looking stern. I liked that fast men
in fast cars were inconvenienced by toads
making their way slowly in straight lines towards the place
where all the sex was happening. I liked that some people
were late because other people knew toads were soft,
small and matterful. I liked that after spawning
every single one of those toads was free
from family ties. I told none of this to the baby.

song of the rescued hen

and once I was the egg laid for my deliverance
and to peck was the shape of my devotion dance

and I stepped from my broken cradle into bright
and they took me to the place of proximity and light

and I laid and I laid and was wretched and I laid
and I wrenched all the feathers from my breastbone in that cage

and all horror was my sorrow and I laid and I laid
and was derelict and broken blinded framework of dismay

and I laid till it was over and they took me to the dust
and I scratch beneath the sky that gives me darkness and I roost

and the rain is my solace falling silent through the wind
and its crystals soft and precious as they break across my wings

and I stand beneath its balm to be healed to be strong
and this will be my freedom and I shall be its song

Canada

Nights when the moon's too heavy
I think about my ovaries – those two
low buildings stuccoed, painted pink,
those warehouses that came with me,
once teemed with tiny half-people, all cute-as,
every one clamouring to call me Mum.
Imagine those fat fists you have to kiss,
the soaring blue of their eyes. Listen,
I won't lie, many times I feared one would
storm in headlong with its big head
and list of equipment. I used to welcome
menstruation, even one time on the up
escalator that exits the Tube, and once
in the bakery section of Asda, and twice
I let my body wave a baby through –
how they thrived, how they grew, see them
shopping and hanging out their wet towels.
Today a sonographer found what she sought
and said, *Yep, everything's nicely shut down
in there.* Think nailed planks over each entry
and exit, in the shape of an X.
Think windows boarded-up, graffiti
scrawled on pink. I'd like to think
the little half-people made it safely out.
I'm picturing them, looking like me
on the Isle of Wight or in Canada. Yes,
that's the place. Say it with me. *Canada.*

Woodland

At the poetry festival, the gorgeous boy poets
are taking turns to read poems about kneeling
in woodland or being knelt before by boys who may

or may not be poets. The girl poets are listening
as girl poets do. Some are aching from sitting
for hours, hearing about the boy poets coming

in woodland without them. Some are thinking
of the winter woodland months, of the cold
or wet, or both and the fact that it might be

totally fucking worth it. Others are thinking
glad thoughts about how lucky they are to be girls
with skirts you can theoretically lift in woodland,

without wet trousers it could be a win win
wet woodland wise. One girl poet has pale legs.
She thinks about the price of tights, of their fragile weave

on the wet woodland floor. She'd like to read
poems about men kneeling for women in woodland
or women kneeling for women in woodland.

She'd like to read poems about women kneeling
for men on a rug in woodland during a warm spell.
She has not read every poem about woodland, if there are

any poems that address the above, then Respect.
She's just saying, she'd like to read of a clitoris
in woodland. She's just saying *vulva,* twice. *Vulva.*

Margate in September

If there's sand and you can let yourself,
what is there to do on a beach but dig?
We dig, the boy and me, with our hands
and the old red spade because it's back to school
tomorrow and back to work tomorrow,
and today the sun still thinks it's June,
spreading loose glory over the sea, over us
with our gorgeous and our ungorgeous bare skin,
and we're pushing ourselves right up to the margin
of the last page of summer, digging an island
as the tide comes in, salt water reaching
to take back what we borrow, and it must be
the boy's thrill that calls the others. Kids,
and tattooed men with shovels. A tribe of diggers,
that's what we are, with a drum'n'bass soundtrack
rising from somewhere, and us digging to the beat,
digging ourselves an island until it's a thing
of greatness with us on top, water all around
in the almost evening, holding our spades,
our ice creams and beer. Everyone together,
not digging now, but thinking our separate thoughts
of all the things scared and incomplete,
here's the marvellous thing we finished.

Candyfloss

I was the kind of mother that said no to candyfloss.
I was the killjoy main bitch, I was Mummy, I was boss.
I kept the dentist's advice handy, up here in my head,
just say no to everything was the gist of what he said.
But there was just this one time at the primary school summer fair,
we were women being willing, we were doing the lion's share.
And they had hired for the occasion, a candyfloss machine
that called for a skilled operative and yours truly was dead keen
so I fastened tight my apron and said hello to the vicar,
you can find him in the church. I knew this would be quicker
so I poured in all the sugar and turned the contraption on
and added red to its rotation. It didn't take too long
for the sugar to melt like cobwebs and fly out in lovely clouds
that perfumed the air of the playground and magnetised the crowds
of little children who rushed over to form an orderly nice queue,
to wait for me, not pushing (this is England, 's what we do).
And I fashioned for every single child a pink cloud on a stick
I winked, I took their money, how they loved me, I was slick.
There was sugar in my eyebrows and sugar in my hair
And though my shift was over, I honestly didn't care,
I stayed inside that apron. I spun sugar all the day,
not even the headmaster could wrench this girl away.
And when I saw, in the distance, my own children looking sad
with their bread sticks and their hummus, their carrot sticks in bags,
I beckoned them and handed them the booty. I was kind,
And they legged it up the sports field just in case I changed my mind.
And deep within my conscience I heard a disapproving cough.
It was only the voice of the dentist. I told him to fuck off.

Mother

Sunday night we watch a documentary
about sea otters. We hear trickling water,

see their drenched salty bodies close up
there on the giant screen of our new T.V.

Those otters are in the room with us,
girl ones holding on tight to their babies

paddling backwards, teaching them how to crack clams
on a flat rock balanced on their furry chests.

They captivate our evening with their wet
whiskers, their closeable ears, their cute

forepaws-free backwards aquatic ease.
It's all in H.D. We see the slick gleam

of salty wet fur, hear their excitable squeaks,
the click of clam on rock. Click and again,

click. *Oh please don't stop.* I'm up on my feet
to punch the air when one sweet legend

of a baby sea otter finally manages to smash a clam
to oblivion, and eats that bivalve mollusc.

My heart is racing, I'm sweating with relief.
I want to phone my friends. I want to ask

all those women: *Can your baby crack clams?*
Are you tired of swimming?

Backwards Tattoo

The plan reversed, a blink, a sudden seamless
u-turn, the garland relaxes its grip, its ramble
over her biceps. Dark stems of waxen ivy,

the brazen crimson peony untether, fall,
her breath an exhalation, awkward.
How her heart sprints as sore unspools.

Soon this artist, his labour, will never have pierced
her warm girl-flesh. The thrill of her flush
will not be his to keep. Rebellion cringes,

shrinks, its flames die back, no ash nor rage
to own what was always hers. Chat rolls home
to her tongue, her throat; words unform, dissolve.

Salt beads of sweat flatten, blood-hued flesh
on bone. This artist's work is now a gift. Tenners
warm again in her jeans, as his hand unveils

the skin's unique terrain. Meticulous
is this untattooing, how he swabs her skin back to itself.
Hers was a whim, reversible. The book she holds

is closed. She turns her head to unsee each page
that blazed with small defiances. Instead this sweet
inversion, to her life uninked, hurt a little less.

Shed

Like a sweet, Scotland is there on your tongue,
melts into words – *lochan, wotter* – please
say them for me. On the long road trip we search

for the headstone of your mother who died
with you but a wee boy. *Dreich* day this –
churchyard grey, your eyes wet green. No trace.

Of all your native words, my favourite is *shed*.
With a wet comb your mummy parted your hair –
perfect white line, a little above one ear.

Smoothed flat, wet over your head's small rise,
well *shedded*, love in the lips that kissed you
and the hands that sent you solo to life.

Palermo

From Italy you send photographs of patisserie.
I learn the names, say them out loud in bed.
Cassata Siciliana. Biscotti di mandorle.
You vouch for their delicate sweetness,
write that the pale green cream is pistachio.
There is icing sugar on your glasses.
I feel your sunshine on my arms,
see you blow froth to reach the coffee.
     After work I scan books of poetry, reading
only the last lines hoping for something
complete. Next door are watching a war film —
gunfire rattles my quiet.
                    Tonight you send
a picture of worn flagstones in a piazza
made pewter by light and rain. So you've had rain.

Therapy

Tuesday evening habit now, to haul
the bruised animal of our couple to a safe place.
We are people faithful to our demographic,

predictable as human foibles, so
separate in our specifics and slightly hung over,
we sling the dislocated animal in the back

and drive to Ian in the Cinquecento.
Ian believes an animal's sorrows
are so objective. We set the creature down

to consider its potential together.
Our collective makes theatre of what is there.
We listen to the animal breathe. I say softly,

you say shallow, Ian says starved of oxygen.
We are glad for the proximity of Ian,
for his voice and how easily it executes

the obvious. The sleeping animal rolls over.
Now we see its shocking vulnerability,
want it to dream of running without hurt,

to know the billowing freedom of certainty.
Sometimes our solutions are silence,
enough to see our animal at peace. Sometimes

we remember it's the only one of its kind.

Pneumonia

We planned to sugar the news – all good things
duplicated. Birthdays, cakes, the garden swing.

Guilt ached in the night, crouched there
braced to spring and the light clicked on, off.

Then, almost ready to tell the kids we'd be loving them
from separate buildings, you fell ill.

Of course, this is the way sickness travels,
on the fault lines of disappointment. I waited

while your fever burned. Sleep took our last days,
until one bright morning I watched you fight

free of the dark and opening brown eyes said it –
I'm still leaving – our hands were touching.

Voiced, I saw healing spark and catch – its crackle
and blaze. In the afternoon you sat up, stretched.

The shower ran for a long time. Years. I heard
the coughing, and then you began to sing.

The song of it

Before I knew the terms and conditions
of love's round gravity I loved a boy at school
and the song of it gathered the world in.

If I quieten the radio fifty years on
I can feel it fire up, deep in my chest,
my heart's fierce engine hum, a lifetime gone

away from the time we whispering agreed
that the shapes in clouds were what we said we saw,
and when a friend was needed he chose me,

and I him. Our love was a living thing we kept,
but mine too flimsy when they taunted him
for poverty and gentleness. How he wept

with gratitude when they upped and ran away
then was gone from school, never to come back.
I have not told of what I lost until today,

perhaps conceding love was smaller then
than now, and perhaps not even love at all,
though, how it hurt to not see him again.

Winters were harder

Rob says winters were harder way back
when for a dare he walked the breadth
of the frozen Thames, tiptoed out, tense
for the crack that never came but gave him
a boyhood marked by this: Peril outwitted.
Courage gripped in the fist and breath
of memory, when the wield and push
of river rush was stilled for one whole week.
Rob says he was chicken. Bank to bank
and back was not risk enough. His mate
hauled his bike, his life to the mid-way,
and cycled the line of its centre in a duffle coat,
singing *look at me Jesus, look no hands.*
At his back, Day's Lock. Ahead, Moulsford,
and here beneath the whole pinched sky,
a boy laughing, feasting on the thrill,
feet on the pedals of a hand-me-down bike.
Below him lidded darkness, iced silver,
thickness unknown all fringed with the living
bones of winter trees, laid out to the far
cold sea. Don't you think a boy's life seen
from here is limitless? Stand on the water
a minute. Now tell me this isn't forever.

This Dog

You did not come here for this dog that belonged to an old person
who hadn't walked her in eight years. At the rescue home they say

this dog has seen only the inside of a small house, with news of outside
shouted from a television. No, this is not the dog you came for.

You want a dog that will run with joy's engine roaring through her being,
a dog who can find the whiff of life, who lifts her nose to breathe it all.

This dog knows nothing of running, of fields unfolding below cathedral skies,
has not heard distant birdsong, nor felt the urgent, jubilant rush to chase it

down from the heavens, and failed, felt her failure, yet whose hope has not faltered,
but been born again, again as if this were the day that running was made.

Nevertheless this is the dog that, from behind a chain-link fence,
sparks a yearning in your chest. A dog who wants you, can hold her gaze,

your gaze, for a long time. This is the dog that comes home with you,
ears flat, unsure in the car. Later this dog will lie with her head on your lap,

the weight of it a thing so complete you will not move. This is the dog
who that first night, frightened, finds her way beneath your warm duvet.

But now you drive this dog to a hill, where wisps of sky call through cloud.
She crouches, wind ruffled, tail down. You unclip her lead, as she sees

the trees nodding towards a fresh rumour of autumn. She lifts her head.
Now the very strings of the soul of this dog tighten, and she runs,

which is when you know that she knows all the moments that came before
have been for this, the one that belongs only to this dog.

Rain

Rain you knew was coming
because the *will it rain today* app
said you could bank on it. Rain
that falls so hard the drains
can't cope. Rain that's silver
and says *right now this road is my river*
then gets down and does it. Rain
that quickens then quietens.
Rain that answers the questions
grass asks. Rain that explains
gravity. Rain that repeats this again
and again like a patient teacher. Rain
that pleases birds. Just listen
to them. Rain that is torrential,
relentless. Rain that is only
tiny aerosol droplets, the kind
of light rain that makes you
really wet. Rain that ruins
and cares nothing for letting up.
Rain that's unexpectedly warm
when you're swimming in
the cold sea knowing for once
you've outwitted it so you
tell this to the sky. Rain
that comes on your birthday
every year and what did you
expect, boy born of a Scottish
autumn? Rain that doesn't
touch us because we're indoors,
listening to its quiet music
of fall, not saying much at all,
and you stayed, and you stay.

Curations

The day comes late summer – you hear the ratchet clicks
of the police car's handbrake, beyond the kitchen window.

The two officers walk up the path, too fast, to tell you that
your son is dead. The woman assumes intimacy, her hand heavy,

awkward on your arm. You can smell milk on her breath.
You'll remember always the sheen on the fabric of her jacket.

The thought of her hovers; how she must be moving through
the minutes of her day, in the evening telling her husband

of the *boy, only 25, who took enough pills to kill a racehorse.*
That's what he typed in. You see the cut potato on her fork,

the lift to her open mouth, the jut of her chin to meet it.
They walk from the house with their dog, her knowing

everything she could have done was gathered up, curated.
And September's here, you can feel it playing with your hair.

What the horses told us

This is how you wait for me – silently in the churchyard with the stones
of those forgotten or remembered in parched flowers and the heart's need to gild.

In your pram you liked the shade. Now you wait beneath your tree
to scan the green of a valley's wet morning. Sometimes I watch the way you walk to me,

when I can't it's because of the loneliness that slings its arm around your shoulders,
settles to the shape of you, its loyal friend.

It's a dead weight. I have no map, nor might to bear it for you. I'm pretty sure
I've never had God but if he were mine I'd give him all to you.

I'll keep today, white hairs like rivulets spreading in your beard, smiling
eyes-down at our tender stories. How the morning braided us together,

autumn rhyming her stride with yours, showing us the places she worked,
her needle threaded red, laughing at the wasted apples we bent to gather.

How the horses took them from us – bit down to taste the juice of what was saved.
How they knew that nothing greater touched this earth.

The demolition of Didcot power station

If you hadn't killed yourself we'd have come up here
together to see the cooling towers demolished.

You would have been the first one awake, would have said *let's go*
and legged it up the hill, the only boy amongst girls.

Now I walk to the highest place and wait. Summer rolls out
her project, yellow fields crouching beneath the cornered day.

The river is stilled and silvery like it's always been from here,
the hills people-dotted. Some carry children in Disney pyjamas,

jiggling them on their shoulders. We face the power station,
then it comes: the gut-boom of the detonation, then the minute pause

as if perhaps it might not happen, as if those three great beasts
might defy the confidence of explosives, of all that planning

and stand unshakeable, dominating the skyline, making clouds
for children just as we once were forever, and into that small,

hopeful space you might slip back no questions asked,
I swear it to you now. Then the drop, the white rim of each tower

a mouth roaring at the sky, each mouth roaring
its silent *no,* as the dust rises to take it down.

Tower

My father took me to London
when my whole fist could fit
inside his palm.

On the Tube he lifted me up
and, holding tight stepped out
from our carriage to the next
through the filthy hurtling dark
to thrill me, then did it again.

By the river he bought chestnuts
roasted on a brazier.

My red gloves swung on strings.
I looked up at the tower of him,
and grief would never dare
to touch my life.

LIVE CANON